The

School

of

Soft-Attention

POEMS

The

School

of

Soft-Attention

POEMS

FRANK LaRue OWEN

HOMEBOUND PUBLICATIONS
Ensuring the Mainstream Isn't the Only Stream

Homebound Publications
Ensuring the mainstream isn't the only stream
WWW.HOMEBOUNDPUBLICATIONS.COM

Published in 2018 • Homebound Publications
Front Cover Image © Trần Anh Tuấn
Cover and Interior Designed • Leslie M. Browning
ISBN • 978-1-947003-96-5
First Edition Trade Paperback

10 9 8 7 6 5 4 3 2 1

Homebound Publications is committed to ecological stewardship. We greatly value the natural environment and invest in environmental conservation. Our books are printed on paper with chain of custody certification from the Forest Stewardship Council, Sustainable Forestry Initiative, and the Program for the Endorsement of Forest Certification.

for doña Río,
who guided me
into the wilderness
of the self, and
the wilderness
of New Mexico

for my mother,
a lifetime student
in the school of soft-attention,
who encouraged me at an early age
to listen to Nature deeply,
to pay attention to dreams,
and to consult the *I Ching*

and

my father,
for river-times
and
"black water cartography"

Contents

~

"Who said my poems are poems?
These poems are not poems.
When you realize that my poems are not poems,
then we can talk of poetry."

—Ryōkan Taigu, Zen hermit-poet

"The third poetry is sometimes never written;
but when it is, it is written by those
who have brought nature and art
together into one thing."

—WALTER INGLIS ANDERSON

Preface
The Dao of Receiving

"A man doesn't go in search of a poem;
the poem comes in search of him."
–YANG WAN-LI

Outside: gray day, dark clouds, white frost on branches.

Inside: I sit wrapped in a blanket beside a rain-dappled window
gazing up at the swaying sentinel pines, contemplating *Dao*.[1]

A black-capped chickadee, adorned with all the same colors of this day,
darts in and out of view. Flowing with the moment, a thought stirs like
feathers ruffling:

Heart-Mind, left to its natural state, is vast as a panorama of Nature.
If settled, receptive, a poem may arrive like the seed-hunting chickadee
flitting through.

A splash of color. A flash of life and movement. A brief moment in this
shared dream. Are we truly present to receive it? This is the path, on this
gray day, and every other day.

Words emerge from the silent illumination of the wordless Dao.
Yet, words can never be complete.

---

1 The Dao, alternately spelled Tao, is a Chinese word that translates as way, path, route, or
living principle. For followers of the Dao, the Dao is intuitive. The Dao is felt and known but
cannot be articulated with mere human speech or words. Indeed, in the first line of the *Dao De
Jing* (Tao Te Ching), a key text of Daoist tradition, it states: The Dao that can be named is not
the Eternal Dao.

Introduction

I often ponder the mysterious phenomenon that is poetry; even more than I write it. From the old Daoist and Chan poets of China and haiku and haibun poets of Japan, who often gazed at mountains and were stirred to brush a poem after sitting in meditation, to modern-day wayfaring, activist, and eco-poets of today, there seems to be a true common denominator among them all. Poetry is inseparable from awareness and spirituality.

Whether I write a poem or not, the practice of inner-outer observation is part of the daily course. It's part of the heart-mind of Dao-trackers. It's inseparable from the Zen mind of tea masters. It's part of the luminous tapestry of indigenous earth-spirit traditions where 'second-attention' is cultivated. It's a current that flows through American eco-poetry and even some of the cowboy poetry of the American West. So, as a lifetime student of consciousness, and a writer of poetry, it is natural to me to see poetry as a path of observation, as a way of working with dreams, as a practice for connecting with Nature. Poetry is one of the indispensable elements of our universal human heritage.

Poetry can also be a means of initiation for both poet and reader, spurring what some Jungians call innerwork. Poetry brings people together into community. Poetry is an experience of consciousness. Poetry is a way of seeing, a way of listening, a way of hearing with the whole body and soul. Poetry is rooted in what Rev. Dr. Joey Shelton calls "holy noticing." From the Mazatec curandera Maria Sabina to the ancient Zen hermit-poet, Stonehouse, all contemplative and earth-spirit traditions and their subsequent expressions of poetry meet at the trailhead of such holy noticing.

In gathering the poems for this book, I circled back around to another idea of poetry held by one of my late teachers, doña Río,[2] who said poetry is "an ongoing curriculum offered by the life around you and within you." Though not a published poet herself, doña Río was a seasoned practitioner of her path of poetry-as-observation. She was a master of paddling her "spirit boat" through the river of heart-mind, guiding others through theirs, and using poetry as a way to process experiences on her unique cross-cultural spiritual path, which was shaped by indigenous/Mesoamerican worldviews and her practice of Zen meditation. If it weren't for her, and other poet-teachers I crossed paths with along the way, like Bill Scheffel and the late Jack Collom, there might not be any poems in this book.

~

I first encountered a poetry that moved me on the cusp of my teen years, nearly four decades ago. It was a verse from the great haiku master of Japan, Matsuo Bashō, author of *Narrow Road to the Interior*, the classic travel journal blending spiritual prose, travel observations, and haiku poetry. Most people who know of Bashō know of his famous poem about a frog leaping into the water, of which there are innumerable translations. The most often quoted in the public domain: *old pond...frog jumps in...sound of water.* That was not the first verse of Master Bashō I encountered, however. It was this one, and it split me open like a gourd:

> "Seek not the paths of the ancients;
> seek that which the ancients sought."[3]

---

2 doña Río (Darion Gracen) was a psychotherapist, writer, wilderness guide, spiritual mentor to many, and life-long student of indigenous and Buddhist wisdom. Her core philosophy. "Open your heart. Awaken your mind. Live the best life you can."
3 A phrase which apparently first appeared in a work attributed to Bashō entitled "Words by a Brushwood Gate" (translator unknown).

When I read these words as a pre-teen, it was not a "normal" reading. It was a lightning strike. The phrase struck and sizzled down my spine and was followed by a gentle sense of relief that washed over me like a cool breeze in summer. Bashō's words woke me from my human trance. I experienced it as a source of direct instruction; a liberating decree from an elder; a personalized sanction to chart one's own course in creative and spiritual matters; a universal outflow of permission to faithfully follow where the soul may lead. As I ponder my approach of the same age that Bashō was when he died in 1694, it strikes me that, in many ways, I owe my whole path of poetry to Bashō. Even though I am not a poet who focuses on his poetic form of haiku (short, three-line poems with a 5-7-5 syllable structure), it is the wandering heart-mind of Bashō to which I am forever grateful, and is one of the spirits that spurs me onward.

When I learned that Bashō trained for a time in Zen, was highly influenced by themes from Buddhism and Daoism, and took daily inspiration from the works and life of a hermit-poet named Saigyō, a wandering Buddhist priest who preceded Bashō by 450 years but whom Bashō earnestly felt was his teacher,[4] I began reading everything I could about Zen, nature poetry, Chinese and Japanese poetic traditions specifically, and the legacy of global mystical, shamanic, and contemplative poetry in general. Soon, fully inspired, I began putting pen to paper myself.

In my late teens, I took up the formal practice of *zazen* (seated meditation of the Zen Buddhist tradition) after reading Shunryu Suzuki's *Zen Mind, Beginner's Mind*, a Zen classic first published in 1970, the year after I was born. Paired with zazen, I also had various experiences in ceremony with First Nations people including Anishinabe, Haudenosaunee, Lakota, Mayans, and Yaqui. Each culture has their own tradition of sacred words, songs, and poetry that affected me greatly. Likewise, I delved into a fre-

---

4 A feature identical with the 18th-century Zen hermit-poet Ryōkan in relation to the 9th-century Chinese poet Hanshan, or Cold Mountain. According to Aikido master, Buddhist priest and translator, John Stevens, Ryōkan would frequently copy Hanshan poems and put them around his hut for meditation.

quent practice of contemplative forest walking (now termed *shinrin-yoku*: "forest-bathing" in contemporary Japanese), an ancient practice being rediscovered today by the medical community but which has always been inseparable from the old Daoist and Buddhist hermit-poets of China, Japan, and Korea.[5] For some reason, I knew instinctively to gravitate to this practice.

In the late-90s, after graduate school, my interest in the interface between mind-training, nonordinary states of consciousness, time in Nature, and poetry took on an added level of dimension and practice. I began a decade of study with an eclectic, somewhat reclusive teacher, whom I had met in Colorado but who had moved to New Mexico. Shaped by her own experiences with Mesoamerican, Native North American, and Japanese Buddhist paths (all traditions in which she studied and trained), doña Río's path was characterized by a profound view of cosmos, Nature, the psychology of transformation, and a deep love of art, poetry, and wisdom wherever it may emerge in the cultures of the world. Doña Río's mentoring of me at her red-earth adobe bungalow on Cerro Gordo in Santa Fe, in the forests and mountains east of the city, and in the arroyos of northwest New Mexico, was a significant influence on my practice of poetry; poetry as eco-poetics, poetry as dreamwork, poetry as earth-spirit experience, poetry as an expression of Dharma art, poetry as a contemplative practice of awareness and attention.

With her death in 2007, however, I suddenly felt like a small bird, with untested wings, kicked from the nest. For years, it felt like I was falling through the air. I had yet to trust the wind. If you had asked me then, I would have reported that I was floundering, drifting like a ghost inside my own life. I felt utterly groundless, and I was grieving.

---

5 Contemplative forest walking, of course, has been practiced by more than a few of the New England transcendentalists and Dharma-Beat poets who would follow in the footsteps of the hermit-poets of old.

I entered a phase of depression—a *Dark Night of the Soul* contemplative Christians call it—from having lost not only a dear friend but also a key reference point on the path I had been walking. Yet, for anyone working with an authentic spiritual teacher or artistic mentor or guide, that teacher will continue turning you back onto yourself rather than allowing you to collapse into the relationship or some kind of overzealous adoration. Spiritual and creative authenticity has no room for codependency; and, so, with doña Río's death, I had nowhere else to go.

I was, once and for all, turned back onto myself. As such, following her teachings and the general markers of the path that she lived herself, I turned inward. I turned to the practice of meditation. I turned to idleness in Nature for healing my grief. I turned to an old Daoist and Buddhist practice used by hermits for thousands of years called the 'Dark Retreat' to seek some sense of stabilization from the painful turmoil I felt. It took me nearly another decade before I began to feel a sense of regaining what doña Río called practice-equilibrium.

Practice-equilibrium is more than a concept; it is a felt somatic experience that informs one's creative and spiritual life. It applies to artists of all kinds including writers, poets, dancers, actors, visual artists, martial artists, yoga practitioners, practitioners of the Way of Tea, and meditators alike. The term does not mean that the hard knocks of life no longer affect the practitioner. Practice-equilibrium isn't a fixed or static state, nor a permanent stage of development. You don't achieve it one day and then go on autopilot. It is work.

Equilibrium, in this sense, is the ongoing practice of mindfully rebalancing when we are thrown off-center. If you're an artist (of any kind), or paying attention to your life (as the artist of your life), then you are a practitioner, and being thrown off-center, especially in the world we live today, is part of the territory, part of the job description of the human experience. If anything, not taking the numbing path of pop-culture distraction of most modernistas, people who work with practice-equilibrium will often find that they feel things even more fully and intensely. We let life in, intentionally. We are the ones who willingly accept the life prescription of Zen master and poet Thich Nhat Hanh who says: "Do not turn your eyes from suffering." To do that, a constant, vigilant practice of rebalancing is needed. In this way, practice-equilibrium is rather more like the consciousness of a seasoned surfer. Conditions change, waves arise, and the practitioner, relying on practices that enable us to stay fully present with our experience, adjusts the "surfboard" of heart-mind.

After nearly a decade of solitary practice after my teacher's death, I have found a refreshed practice-stride with all of the practices I studied with her, including poetry. With it has come full comprehension of something she was fond of saying. This comprehension arrived in similar fashion as the "lightning strike" of Matsuo Bashō's verse about "seeking what the ancients sought."

I opened an old journal of mine and found a quote of doña Río's I had written down (of which there are many):

"Even when you feel lost, you are never not on the path."

Having taken after my late teacher, I've lived as a hermit-poet for over a decade now, "down in the city, behind the courtyard wall," as some of the old Daoist and Chan poets who followed this same pattern might've said. I am ever-oriented to the unique cross-pollinated creative and spiritual path my teacher shared with me, and this is often reflected in my poetry. I have come to think of this ongoing curriculum as 'the school of soft-attention.'

Ultimately, whether writing one of my own poems, or steeping in the words of someone else in this unofficial cross-cultural lineage of crazy clouds and wayfarers, it is a thoroughgoing path of sourcing within the flow of the Great Transformation of life, slowly finding a sense of peace inside one's own skin. I hope some of the poems in *The School of Soft-Attention* can support you, dear reader, in doing the same. Perhaps one of them will inspire you to turn toward your life in a new way, with a new way of looking, a new way of seeing, a new way of paying attention to the seen and unseen life within and around you.

Frank LaRue Owen
near the Natchez Trace
Michiziiibi (Mississippi)

When Your Spirit Eyes Are Tired

You have two sets of eyes
the physical ones
and the vast eyes
placed within you
by the spirit land
through which you move.

You may think
the rocks and trees from your land of birth
are just rocks and trees of your land of birth

but your second set of eyes are on loan from them
and unseen fearless things around you
that you can never fully understand.

If you awake one day
with tired spirit eyes,
pay heed;
that's a different type of fatigue
a signal arriving
from your own ground of being
telling you in no uncertain terms
that a big rusted lock
is about to be busted open within you.

The question The Teacher will ask
on the path between mountain top and parking lot:

Are you brave enough
to embrace what awaits
on the other side of the door?

Forest Bathing

There is a way of entering the forest
when the breeze of the trees
becomes your guide

when the cool gray-green days
and humid blue-green nights
become your own skin

where the unfurling paths
through the emerald light
become flowing streams.

Paths as luminous rivers
for your two uncovered feet,
salmon-like and aching,
to work out their
strange haunted yearning
for a home
whose vista
they haven't yet seen
yet somehow know
just the same.

There is a way of approaching the self
without a heavy hand
when the heart-mind
slowly becomes unburdened by the past,

where the body
listening with the whole of itself
finally becomes attuned
to all the subtle happenings
in the realm not yet stained
by the faithless world of man.

Cradle of Sunlight

I went to the well tonight to draw water
looked over the edge, down into the darkness
that has always been a reliable mirror,
a quencher of deep thirsts.
It was empty.

At first, it made me think of my Irish ancestors
and all their striving and starving and yearning and stories...
of how old wells could run dry
and the underground rivers that fed them
could 'Up and Move'
if someone hadn't honored them, properly.

I wondered what ancient river inside of me
I had ignored for the water of life to run dry on a rainy night.

Then, I realized the vision wasn't about me.

Like the Hawk of Achill taking flight,
the eyes of my heart-mind were whisked up
on the high winds of night.

I was carried across nine glowing waves
and shown a moment in time
when life made more sense;
when there was a magic order to things
and every moist day was saturated in mystery.

I needed to see that, freshly, to be able to see you, clearly.

Time has passed.
You've taken your warrior-self on another adventure.
Tenacious. Beautiful.
Fighting your way through as usual.
And now I know,
that this place is the empty well
and you are the life-giving river that has moved on
because you were not honored here.

This is not a poem...even though you asked for one.
It is a katana-prayer slicing through air.
My deepest wish for you
is that the deepest parts of you
can one day put down the battle
and let yourself truly be held
in a cradle of loving sunlight.

Reincarnation Halfway Through A Life

Four decades leaning forward.

Skin stretching over bone.

Following a message planted long ago.

A drowsy lion
chasing after mirages
until a cold and misty New Year night.

I'm sure I appeared to be a man
climbing out of the wreckage.

I was a newborn
emerging from a womb.

Back When - April 22, 1591

I was sitting on a rough-hewn bench
eating a meager meal
in a small roadside saké shop.

A large jar of saké sat in front of me.

I ate, I sipped, I watched:

...an ant walk across the table

...rain *drip-drip-dripping* down a rain-chain

...the *shuffle-shuffle-swish* of a fine lady in late Spring kimono.

Two women at a nearby table,
maybe sisters, maybe aunt and niece,
gossiped.

Disturbing news rippled through the village.

Sen no Rikyū had committed seppuku[6].

---

6 Seppuku: Ritual suicide, literally "cutting the belly." We've all had a dream from which we awake when the emotional residue of the dream stays with us. This poem is based upon such an experience. The contents are linked to historical events, namely the ritual suicide of Sen no Rikyū, a Zen man and cultural influencer of the Way of Tea. Rikyū had been a confidant to Toyotomi Hideyoshi, a daimyō-samurai, and had also served as his tea master. No one knows why, but Hideyoshi ordered the tea master to take his own life. On his last day alive, Rikyū held a tea ceremony, gave his tea equipment away to the assembled guests, and brushed a Zen death poem before committing *seppuku.*

I awoke from the dream, crying, openly,
in this life,
having comprehended
the profound teaching
lost on tyrant Hideyoshi.

Tapestry

My first teacher taught Letting-Go Mind.
She was human, very human,
but also a woman
made of thunder and lightning.

Her slate-gray robe
and long strand of mahogany-red neck beads
placed her centuries before
despite what the calendar said.

Toward the end, she pulled out an unmarked box.
From it, she pulled a map.
'The World,' it said
which I read
as she spread
the tattered brown paper across the table in front of us.

Enso[7]-like circles
made from wine stains
covered the map.
Clearly, late night discussions
had occurred over it.

Spirals inside of smaller circles
covered the world, East and West, North and South.

---

7 Enso: A quick, spontaneous painting of a circle, usually with one stroke of black ink, that represents enlightenment.

Without speaking, my eyes made their own inquiry.
Seeing this, she nodded and slowly
moved her hand over the unfolded paper.

"A network of courtyards, linked,
dedicated to The Way," she announced.
"Each one has a Keeper. In time, you will visit them.
In time, you too will become
a Tender of the Long-Night for others."

My new teacher teaches No-Adding-To Mind.
She is not human,
but rather the rain of summer
falling from the edge of the roof.

True Name

The small hermit lives on a mountain.
The great hermit lives in town.
-Chinese proverb

This morning
like a fresh drop of blood
flowing from a newly-scored wound
"Red-Shield" made his appearance.

The bright-winged cardinal
who faithfully visits to wake me each day
brought the same instruction
as that old Nangchen poet:
'First Thought, Best Thought.'

As my eyes opened onto a pink dawn
peeking through the dark pines
I settled softly into myself.

The Heart-Mind became its own scribe.

I am a long way from the cultured days
when I was a mountain dragon among the pines;
but like the old days
I feel like a culture of one
a visitor dwelling in a province
where they don't speak my tongue.

With exertion and practice my eyes have become
clear of the world's red dust again.
I have penetrated the veil of time's illusion.
I am an ancient mountain temple
hidden inside the body of a man.

Namo

I. What's In A Name?

A voice mumbled across the table in the tavern,
with a subtle hint of disdain:
"So, what's with this name?"

I said something about poets, and teachers of poets,
poet-names and Dharma names.

I started to talk about people
who follow these old traditions
of being and naming,
like my teacher,
and how the names placed in front of us
are like horizon lines to aim for.

I started to mention the tapestry of waking-dreamers before us;
how Tao Yuanming, at mid-life, became Five Willows
how Bai Juyi left the city and would only answer
to the name "First Mountain"
how Matsuo named himself Sobo, then Tosei, then Bashō
how Buson took his dead teacher's poet-name,
Yahantei, Midnight Studio
how Otagaki Todo, after a whole life of loss,
gave herself the name Lotus Moon
and stayed hidden within the town,
writing poetry,

firing pottery,

moving every year

as if she lived on the surface of a stream.

I stopped myself, knowing full-well I cannot convey

this multidimensional mandala

of oversouls and lush places of memory.

So, I just left it at:

My teacher gave it to me.[8]

II. Walking Toward Something – Not Running Away

How do you explain the poet-name?

Will it be a nourishing feast

or a kettle of rotten fish to the listener?

How do you articulate the age-old practice

of trading-in ego concerns

and Floating World grasping and greed

---

8 This poem is about the practice of taking-on names either for creative or spiritual reasons, a common practice in Buddhism, in Chinese and Japanese artistic traditions, and in indigenous earth-spirit / medicine traditions. My whole life I've been known by different names. My father has always called me *Pancho* (a Spanish variant of Frank). My late maternal grandmother always called me *Lobo* (Spanish for wolf). At one point, in my Zen training, I was given a Japanese name. Names, in this way, can be like a horizon line one travels to, or a creative "horse" that takes you there.

all in service of filling oneself up
with the guiding spirit of the seasons?

What poem can be written, or story told,
that conveys Dawn-Light Clarity
this stepping beyond
this stepping into poems
this making room for the memory-flow
this making space for dead teachers to have their say
this wandering with long-gone poets who are still teaching The Way
this daily guarding of oasis-like spaciousness
for those moments when life-changing conversations
need to take place?

How can it be described
that multi-verse travel
is not only possible
but happening all the time,
all while you,
the poet,
are trying to maintain a body
in the here-and-now?

III. Our True Name Is Found in the Dawn Light

You have to present yourself to the morning.
The whole lot of yourself.

The bags under your eyes.
The pain from being betrayed.

All the things you were meant to give birth to
which you aborted for a half-lived life.
The travel-worn lines in your heart, hands, and face.
The scars and burns and multiple brandings
from being made an exile.
Bring it all.

Whether shy to the light or broken-winged,
you have to present yourself to the morning
and give her your everything.

Only then, will you be given your true name.

From seed-catchers
to sandpipers
bottom-feeders
to dragonflies clicking through the sunbeams,
all are after only one thing:
one humble taste of The Flow.

After offering your "self" to the morning
the night is where you receive your True-Self back.

This is when you learn about the Long View;
that the only mountain you need to climb is yourself
and everywhere
there is a great Circle of Solace waiting;
you just have to be fully present
in that moment
and enter from there.

A Precious Unfurling Evening

Spring night in winter.

The door open to night air.

A family walks by.

A child laughs with glee.

Night-Sit.

I ponder an old phrase of Ikkyū's[9]:

"The buddhadharma is also the Way of Tea."

A bolt of lightning splits my brain open

and I pour down into my own heart.

---

9 Ikkyu Sojun (1394-1481) is one of the most beloved Japanese poets and Zen masters.

Origins

He asked me,
as if looking
for one definitive moment in time:

How did Zen begin?

I pondered the matter a moment.

"Some say it started with a flower held up in the air,
but you can't rely on formulas.
Zen man Ikkyū
was enlightened
by the sound
of a squawking crow."

Coupling

Why fill your nights
with door-slamming conflict

when your bride
could be the gentle falling rain...

your husband
could be the ancient songs
emerging from a dharma-realm
of crickets and night-herons
hidden in a grove
of moon-lit bamboo?

Invisible Belonging

Stop spinning
on your busy wheel of pain
long enough to hear this:

You are not outside the fold
of your original preciousness.

Even the dawn-bird
is heralding this truth
each morning

singing to you a map-song
with coordinates
leading to your renewal.

Even when it seems
you have gone over the edge, falling,
you are woven in.

When family, lovers, friends
are separated by a great distance

the Old Way tells us
to converse through the moon.

Sliding a key
into the lock of memory
you can see
you are never not on the path.

Open heart
open door
wide-open expanse.

With such openness
even long-ago ancestors
can send messages through time

and grandmotherly kisses
can arrive
through the moon
in your teardrop.

The Old Code of Good Travelers

If you're tired of spinning:
anchor.

If you're tired of being pulled
into dark waters of suffering:
stop biting honey-covered hooks.

If you're tired of shouldering heavy weight:
off-load what isn't vital
and begin what is.

Make the sunrise a temple.

Embrace the moon as companion.

Allow the peaceful sounds
of the creatured-night to enter you,
to remind you
of your own
undomesticated atmosphere.

Place the Heart-Mind's Trustworthy Light
onto the Old Code of Good Travelers:

The antidote to depression is devotion.

The Bouquet of the Last Direction

When the soul becomes unburdened
it's like a new saddle on a fresh horse.

Suddenly the trail feels right again,
and the strong horizon line in front of you as you turn
becomes its own form of soothing medicine.

Something of the sting and burn of the old poison may linger
but having crossed over from the Shadowlands into new open territory,
one can almost pick up the scent of blooming flowers within.

You start to notice all the things you hadn't been
all because you'd been so bound up
with the echoes of losses and hauntings.

You know you're ready when ghosts
start chanting from the edge of your life:
Traveler! Good Traveler!
Your 'Crying for a Vision' Time is over.
Time to re-inhabit the Human World!

Then, the simplest of the ten thousand things
start to reach out to you to welcome you home again.

The Morningstar.

The blue sky with its utter completeness.
The serrated clouds coming over the rising pine-covered hills.
Even the food tastes better in the Land of the Great Eastern Sun.

You may find the wandering wild animal of your heart
is somehow more free to travel back through time…
…to pick back up with sources of beauty
and power you had put down.

And maybe, just maybe,
you'll see yourself now
through your childhood eyes
and you'll stand forgiven and realize
the magic you had then never left you;
you just forgot how to listen.

Cosmology

There is a Great Story

that binds us all together

and it's not the one

any of us grew up with.

The Second Bloodstream Sermon

Shakyamuni held up a flower.
Mahakasyapa smiled.

Bodhidharma wandered
rebuffed an emperor
sat in front of a cave wall for nine years.

Dazu cut off his own arm to apprehend the Dharma.
Seven hundred moons later, he was put to death.
He had become the body of the Dharma itself.

Jianzhi stayed to the mountains
avoided all things worldly
combined Buddha and Dao.

Daoxin cut through everything with "Mind and Buddha are one."

Farong the Hermit lived on wildflowers
that small birds brought to him
and dropped into his lap.
When he became a buddha,
the birds moved on.

Hongren the Old managed to plot his own rebirth.
Upon his return, Hongren the Second
looked up Daoxin the Old

so he could continue studying The Way
with his beloved teacher.
Shitou of the Stones
simmered down the Great Matter
into a broth.
When you drink it, you hear him say all over again:
"Neither stained, nor pure,
Heart-Mind stands outside
of birth and death."

Hui-Neng pounded grain with a stone
then cracked open the minds of the masters
with a single poem.
His One Practice Way
set every common task
as a means toward the lantern-lit mind.

So, stop delaying your chores
and putting off the laundry.

Mazu roared like a lion
to help us all walk like one.

Liangjie caught it while crossing a stream.
He had sought it from others his whole life,
but his own face gave it back to him.

We're the same.

Even our own bloodstream
is trying to show us our place
in the great fold of churning stars.

Enjoy your time
in the mirror
tomorrow morning
but be sure to stop and ask:

Who is it
really
that is looking back?

May These Words Drive You Up a Wall

Somewhere within you is a wall.

Clearly you needed a fortress once.

On it is a stain, a watermark,
left over from some great flood you have known.

Whatever it was, forgive it.

It was trying to drive you up and over the wall;
to remind you
to lift up
that lovely beseeching voice you once had.

The one that connects you to you.
The one that makes things happen.

It was just trying to drive you up and over the wall
to show you
that the days of walls and fortresses are over.

The magic of your larger blooming life
has been trying to reach you;
pouring through the cracks
seeping up through the ground around you.

It has no aim, save one: to save you;
to bring back the moist oasis
of midnight wine and pillow talk
to that dry desert you've become.

Prescriptions

Now walk,
especially among the trees if you can.

Matsuo Bashō and Kierkegaard
frequently relied upon this prescription.

Sit for an hour without interruption.
View it as surfing or riding waves in a small boat.
Better yet, view thoughts as clouds
and become the Great Sky of Mind.
This was Jia Dao's way.

Brew a cup of tea. Yunnan Gold or Matcha.
Watch a chickadee dine on a feast of seeds
you put out with your own hands.

Read verses of Lady Momoko Kuroda, Rengetsu, Mary Oliver.
They restore faith, faithfully.

Read a few key phrases of Suzuki Shosan;
take them to heart as if you're being sent on a secret mission.

Don't underestimate how one's living space affects heart-mind.
It is like water. Does yours flow, or is it like a stagnant pond
birthing a hell realm of gnats, mosquitos, fruit-flies, and clutter?

Whatever you do, bring your full breath to it.
Shallow breathing means you are more dead than alive.

Grab three coins.
Toss them six times.
Consult the *Book of Changes*
while listening to crickets, frogs, and rain.

Ponder for a moment that there is, in fact, a world beyond saving;
that it is here, now, cascading swiftly toward its predictable end.

Alongside it, also here-now,
is another world,
bright,
eternal.

Be part of that one.

Leaving No Trace

Wide-open all along,
this hallowed midnight thoroughfare
stirs discussions of the ancient Way;
the one that goes from the Mirrored-Eye
to the deep caverns of the heart
and back out to the cosmos turning-in on itself.

The old instruction still stands:

Be full-of-care what you cast your eyes upon.
Ignore that which does not help you or the world to bloom.

Someone remarks that this time
feels like she's throwing pearls before swine.

The Teacher says:
Stay close and guard your heart-mind in this age of decline.
The Heart-Mind-River knows which way to flow.

So, friend, you are just a crazy cloud like the rest of us;
part of this tribe of foolish beings passing through.

Who's keeping score?
Fade over the horizon, anonymous!

It matters not
if others realized
you were really the rain
falling on their parched and thirsty fields.

Dispensation

after Hafiz, and a night of wine

O, Honey Eyes,
don't leave the house wearing that.

That clunky bag of stones
you're wearing on your shoulders
will never be in season.

Shoulders are not Should-ers.

I know the camel driver
constantly hit you with sharp words
when you were young

but he has moved on
and now you are the one
with the whip in your hand.

Two Zen Poems
When I Gave Up My Robes
and Put My Cowboy Boots Back On

I. The Quenching of the Oldest, Most-Thirsty Part

It is possible
to quench
the oldest
most-thirsty part.

Giving up senseless gossip
that dries out your mouth
is the first step.

Becoming still and quiet is The Way.

Then you become a river
that quenches others every day.

II. There is Never a Place Where the Work Isn't Happening

Search beyond
four walls
and a roof.

Seek
a wider sense
of housekeeping.

Weather Report

When you are part of the caravan of crazy clouds
you start to become a little less domesticated
and a little more like wild mountain weather.

Allegiances shift from the outer to the inner
and when the rains come
you drop everything
to worship the silence found within it.

When you get too much of the world on you
that which is natural in you starts to struggle.

This is when rivers freeze and land turns barren.

This is when thirsts develop that can never be quenched.
This is when life-force stagnates
and the sparkle in your eyes
that others have come to rely on
can fade.

They don't teach this
in churches and synagogues,
mosques and temples.

The best of them want to soothe you from the aches of the world.
Some want to lull you back to sleep.

Others want to hammer you into their shape
so you will behave and keep your mouth shut.

But the old mystery schools and rustic enclaves
of dervishes, curanderas, and Zen women know:

There's a form of nourishment
that only you can give to yourself
and if you don't learn the language
of how that's done,
even on your last day here
you will have remained a stranger to yourself
and all those with whom you kept company.

The Perfumed Breeze
written 33,000 feet over Abiquiú

If your first meals were taken
with the helpless
the hapless
rageful withholders of the Great Love Spark
you can be pardoned...for a while...
for reaching out to the wrong crowd.

A thirsty soul will drink most anything.
False, tasteless company
can seem like sturdy shelter in a sandstorm.

The empty promise of their elixirs is well known.
Once your eyes have cleared,
if you keep drinking their poison
can you really keep blaming them
for continuing to serve it to you?

The Teacher says: Seek softer company now.

There is a whole world hidden inside this one.

The quiet faithful are showering in The Presence,
creating new gardens of belonging
behind city walls

out in the jungle
deep in the mountains
preparing for the return
of the Many-Becoming-One.

Medicine

The look on your face
is one I have seen in my own mirror.

I know you didn't think
you would feel this tired at this age
but this is just a phase.

You're in-between lives within this life.

As the old woman used to say out in Peyote Land:
'Right on time, deary. Right on time.'

For now,
in the place beyond words
just know:
breathing is enough.

The world falls away in silence.

Whoever is secure enough
to let you enter the quiet-dark without them
is your ally.

Whatever is left standing
after your simmering 'death-sleep'
is faith-worthy.

In these times
when even a simple day
can feel like a firing pin

stretching corpse-like
upon the earth
is not leisure.

It is medicine.

The Veiled Pulse of Time

The sting you feel inside your heart
has been there since birth.

We all felt it in our first moments.

It's why you cried out with your mother
breath and blood together

the Needle of the Sun
stitching you
by your grandmother's hand.

The sting you feel inside your heart
has been there
since you first opened your eyes.

Even now,
as we sit watching another sun
step up to her throne,
we can hear the ancient pang in everything.

It cries out just as it did on your first day:
Teach me to speak the language
where there is nothing left to say.

Once Through

Once through, contentment.
Once through, ripe seeing.
Once through, words are nothing
but falling blossoms
and mud on your shoe.
Once through,
the breeze through the leaves, a symphony;
dinner in your bowl, the broth of the sea.
Once through,
there is nothing
to fall back on
for explanation
except a soft gaze
a hello
an embrace
a goodbye.
If you open your mouth
a hungry lioness
will eat your heart
and 108 dragon ancestors
will burn out your tongue.
Not stepping through; no option at all.

Offerings

I wept tonight
with the earth weeping rain

for all that's been lost
and all that is the same.

Then the sky filled
with bullet-like hail

and I ate the icy offerings
like a warrior's last meal.

Embrace

With the high clouds
hugging close to the treetops

the pine and spruce
hugging close to the mountain

the hawk and osprey
hugging close to upper branches

the starling and wren
hugging close to lower branches

the red-wing blackbird
hugging tight to the swaying cattail stalk

the deer hugging close
to the mist of the high grass meadow

it would seem
we are the only ones
who have forgotten the way
of holy embrace.

Hawk of the Pines

Like missing a long lost relative
I realized this morning
I did not hear cicada song.

Instead my ears were filled
with the shrill cry of Matsu no Taka—Hawk of the Pines
piercing the air with secret poet names
and the names of invisible guides.

He does this each year
on the first truly cold day of the season.

Copper beams of autumn light dance across his plumage.
Small birds scatter from his line of flight
then resume their tree-branch gossip in his great wake.

And each year I am left grateful
breathing in the cool air flowing through the screen;
the gray-blue sky
and burnt-umber branches
reminding me of my dual citizenship.

This Way of Seeing

The soul is not a land-locked entity.

It can grow feathers.

Given a scent trail of tea or rice wine
sweetgrass or rose jam

and the one that has me
can follow the aroma of soil
to where the feast of ancients
is still happening in a cathedral of pines.

I do not know the solutions
to this world's great ailments
of pain and power run amok

but I do know
the way of the feathered soul
and I sit like a watchful child
as mine takes wing
and flies into things
and comes away
with greater understanding.

There Is Only One Poem

One day these words will be gone.

So will the hands that sculpted them
and the eyes of mind that saw them
and the pulse of heart
that beat their shapes
on the anvil of vision.

The only echo of what is found here
will be found out there
in the rain
the wind
the tide pools at dawn
a quiet, crackling fire beneath the moon
the song of the surf coming in
the lilting morning talk on the Red Line heading to town
and...the sound of your own breathing.

Listen.

Listen in every place that you are.

Hear.

Hear the laughter of a child
an owl at night
the comforting, domestic clank

of dishes at your morning breakfast.
Hear them as the true poetry that they are.

Then you'll realize: there has only ever been one poem.

There has only ever been one poem
and all poems are but a mirror of that one.

Then you will understand the Great Poet
whose poem is still being sung into Being each day.

Then you will understand that your life
and even your death
is a line in that poem.

Ancient Architecture

By day,
a hired retainer.

By night,
small, bird-like meals
in a ghostly saké house.

Memories unwind.
Multiple lifetimes.
Ancient verses flutter across eyes
like Shinto prayer flags
tied to swaying branches
in the mountains.

Confucian verses stiffen the spine.
Pure Land verses open heart-mind.

And to think:

This was a fire stoked again
all because Ian Fleming
re-acquainted a child
with the architecture
of ancient Japan.

The Seed, The Gate, The Path

THE GATE

I know it seems hard to grasp
but it's about opening your hand
reaching for the Cup of Truth
hidden within your silent life.

Hand the script back to the director of the drama;
tell the playwright to cease adding words to the page.

Dare to be alone
to meet yourself for the first time, really,
realizing that unless you enter the life of your Great Story,
no one and nothing around you
can ever really offer you
a gift worth receiving.

It's about pulling back the curtain
revealing what you've long hidden in shame
and coming to understand for yourself
how it was always a treasure.

It's about comprehending
the hard-edged fact
that if you don't love yourself
enough to take care of yourself
no one

can ever trust you
when you tell them
that you love them.

THE PATH

It all started as a seed
beneath the World Tree;
every tree is the Bodhi Tree[10]
if you are sitting there properly.

It was there that he sat,
and was tested, and challenged,
until he cast off the husk of the self.

From there a seed was passed
across time and great distances,
from hand to hand.

When the seed was planted at Koyasan,
a golden mandala bloomed;
a resting place for flowers thrown.

When the seed was planted at Kailash,
turquoise-colored birds
with flowing red scarves in their beaks
began flying East;
the true governors of Shambhala.

---

10 The Bodhi Tree is the legendary tree Siddhartha sat beneath when he became a buddha.

When the seed was planted at Angkor Wat,
even the roots of the trees cried out:
"Liberation!"

When the seed was planted
atop Linh Son Mountain,
the moon and sun held council,
and drank tea.

Now the seed,
that simple seed,
drinks from the earth out on Beara's land,
deep in the dreaming Catskills.

The seed has been passed.

It is small, and indestructible,
but easily lost.

The seed contains a map.
The map leads to a gate,
and the gate to a path.

Here,
open
your
hand.

Behind All of This

Traveling in crow-form last night
I went upward and outward
beyond this borrowed corpse.

I saw a luminous sight
unfolding like a song
in the lattice of the night.

I saw each of us
our lives
our plans
whatever they may be

linked together
by a giant loom
and by a weaver
whose face we cannot see.

A Cool-Blue Returning
dream poem #52

I am a child.
I am in a great house of many rooms
with large verandas and long hallways.

Relatives are visiting, and friends,
and it is night,
and they are all sleeping.

I rise from my bedding
and move through the cold air
and blackness
until I see moonlight shining
on the white pebbles outside.

I push my way past manicured pines
wisteria
bougainvillea
plum
until my soft feet reach the boundary line.

I make my way out into the forest
for what I know will be my last breath.

Somehow, despite my young age, I have already 'seen';
I have already come into full understanding
that grasping is futile, and thus the reaching too.

I step over and through and lay myself down.
Before my last breath,
I carve a death-poem into a downed tree:

Nature always wins in the end.

As I slowly begin losing consciousness,
easing into what feels like a cool-blue departure,
my traveling-mind flows back through time
to where clouds dream of rain
rain gives birth to rivers
and mountains were our temples.

Though I know it isn't on me,
I feel a weather-beaten Chán[11] robe
gray and tattered and frayed
against the cobalt-blue night.

I think to myself:

'How is it that its shape and weight and stitch and length
is even more familiar than this skin I have now?'

Suddenly I hear the song of a dawn warbler
and all of my memories flow together
like prayer beads on a single strand.

I dreamed I was enlightened
but then I woke up.[12]

---

11 *Chán* is the Chinese equivalent of Zen.
12 A contemporary *koan* shared by Sir Jeremy Eisler.

In the Hour Before Sleep

to someone I have yet to meet

The festival is over.

We sit quietly
sipping on memories of the day
looking out
past window boxes
at revelers heading home.

I turn
and watch
as hieroglyphics
flow from your mouth.

Ancient architectures
are being released again
from doorways
opening up and down your spine.

In this hour before sleep, we feel it.

The fibers
holding the world together
are crackling again.

Practice-Ground

Talking of Practice Over Saké
with the Householder Bright Mountain Forge

In the early afternoon, I lost myself for hours
watching the slow winding roll
of the sun's golden hem edging the clouds.

In the late hours, I met up with Bright Mountain Forge
a householder,
traveling through the region on business,
heading home to the West.

Though his eyes were bright
his belly happy and round from feasting
his beard long and full in the Daoist-style,
his heart seemed stone-like, heavy.

He spoke of marriage, children, the Way of the Householder[13]
precious memories and gifts he would never trade.
But he also spoke of mourning things;
things that would not come to pass
midway through his householder's life.

---

13 Although modern media often depicts Buddhists as monks and nuns, the fact of the matter
is the vast majority of Buddhists in the world are not monastics but are Householders—a family
layperson with a family and job living in society. This is contrasted with practitioners who take
neither the monastic path or the householder path and remain either a hermit or a wander-
ing ascetic. In some Buddhist traditions, a person may transition a number of times between
monastic, householder, and wanderer.

He explained that no one understood this grief,
which could break through any time,
without a moment's notice.
He said everyone he knew sang the same chorus:
You have it all. What else is there?

Knowing that I currently 'live-into the call'
to long draughts of solitude and wandering,
he formally requested I "keep on keeping on"
and not lose my "practice-vigor."

"Practice for practice sake," he said,
"practice for yourself
in memory of our teachers
for a world that needs wisdom and beauty;
but think of me in your practice, too,
and when you doubt it, please push through."

I nodded with deep understanding,
having mourned my own list of things
that don't seem to be in the stars for this life.
I spoke of the Hermit Way,
moving from bright gleaming idleness to movement to poetry,
then into nights of dimly-lit Silent Illumination.

But I also told of my own visit to the stations of mourning
including grieving some of the very things
that are part of his daily practice-ground.

I replied:

"Practice for practice sake
practice for them
practice in memory of the lineage of householders
practice for a world that needs wise children and beauty;
but think of me in your practice, too,
and when you doubt it, please push through,"

We parted that night, hearts gladdened,
feeling a new spark of solace
for who, what, where, and how we are.

He resumed his journey on the road.

I resumed my meditations beneath the stars.

Almond Eyes

I met her in a bakery.

The Andalusian sun had driven me into the shade.

The place was owned by her family.

The aroma of fresh-baked-everything
echoed off the walls like music.

Her father, a Moroccan from Fez,
buzzed from table to table with a smile
like a bee hunting nectar.

She and I sat side by side,
sweaty thigh-to-sweaty thigh, in fact.

Mint tea was our drink by day.
Tempranillo by night.

We talked of lineage, recipes;
exchanged glances and winks
and quotes of Tagore.

One day, I threw a smooth line on her as a test.

When she winced with scolding analysis
instead of gushing like a fluttery schoolgirl,

I knew she had the old soul of a Traveler.

I backed up and explained.

She nodded with knowing and poked my ribs with a smile.

Her little brother put a soft hand on my tattooed arm.

He giggled and asked me to mop the floor; also a test.

I smiled, took the mop in hand,
and spent a long season learning
how love is what makes the dough rise,
not yeast.

Confluence

As the spice boats
stitch their way downriver

their glowing red parasols
and prayer-drenched tassels
shake like dancer's hips.

Children run along the shoreline
stopping only occasionally
to exchange world-changing secrets.

The wind and water here
are no less in conversation.

Seeds
poems
smiles
blossoms
dreams.

The ancient song of sunlight
is drawing the best and brightest
out of everything today.

Tasavvuf[14]

dream poem #17

I awoke in the middle of the night again
enveloped in your fragrance.

Vetiver, rose jam, mint.

Disoriented, my eyes struggled to adjust.

Though I was back in the world of grasping again,
I was no longer of it.

My soul
had pledged allegiance
to something unseen
without my knowing it.

I stumbled like a love-drunk fool through the streets.

Detractors surrounded and mocked me.

Some threw rocks,
others, daggers.

But the Great Traveler
who used my body for shelter
could only laugh.

---

14 Tasavvuf is a Persian word for Sufism.

I still wonder to this day
if they really knew
who was doing the laughing.

Quantum Travel

Elbows on marble
smoke of añejo on the throat
two whirly-gig blondes, bright eyes blinking,
desperately try to get my attention.
I guess they don't realize I'm old enough to be their father.

The only thing on my mind is the soft blue smoke of the dark red hills;
soaking in the soft blue water, just up from Horsethief Canyon,
the last time I remember a smile on your face.

The stars were like jewels.
So were your eyes.
We drank nigorizake[15] like two crazy clouds
that had broken out of prison.
I can't seem to put the memory down.

I pull myself back 'into the now'
and watch the endless scurry around me.
Wandering eyes glancing
wanna-be princesses prancing
jaw-jutting male peacocks strutting
not realizing they're dining in the poison jungle.

I wander home in a trance, pondering:
What is the point of this chaos;

---

15 A creamy, unfiltered style of Japanese saké.

this fast-paced fetishism
this new floating world's religion of freneticism?

I close my eyes in this world
and open them in another.
I cross paths with Hawkeye in spirit-form.

We're wandering through the canyons out from Bandelier,
somewhere between Sanchez and Hondo.
The Rio Grande is a stone's throw...and so we do.

We start skipping stones
and talking about the journey of this life.
His regrets. Mine. Wounds. Time.
Two hawks circle above
and I think to myself, 'What a perfect day.'

I turn and look my father in the face
and find myself thinking
how young he looks for his age.

It occurs to me:
The weight of the heartbreaks we carry
is the only aging force there really is.
It's why we meet some people in their nineties
whose spirits are lighter than eiderdown

and some twenty-somethings
who already seem old,
like they're carrying inhabited dungeons
of banished travelers on the inside.

I awake.

It's the first day of autumn
and my first thought of the season
is the work of off-loading useless cargo.

The ground ahead is a mix of rocky and soft
and a bunch of added weight will do nothing
but sink wagons in deep ruts of mud and regret.

Black Water Cartography
a poem in honor of my father
for the week of his 71ˢᵗ birthday

There is a lot they didn't tell us upon arrival.
This mutual coming-to-terms with such truths…
…what do we call 'that'?

There is a lot you couldn't teach me along the way
because no one was there to teach you.

No one
to initiate us
into the oldest language there is.

No one to point at the gifts and measures
and lacerations of a given moment
and then to say:
You need to remember this.
This is shaping your future self.

No one to ask the great question
of all starting quests:
How is it with your soul
before you begin this new chapter?

There is a lot they didn't tell us upon arrival.
There is a lot we didn't learn along the way
that could've saved time,

and pain,
and other people's pain;
how the maps and paths
and compass-checks,
how the tannin-dark water
turning in on itself,
were all whispers of future terrains
we would come to know
intimately from the inside-out.

Yet, when I really uncoil
this feathered soul
and send it back to when
we were most 'in our element,'
there were river-paddles in our hands.

We were charting something, even then.

We glided along the river in pure synchrony.
We ducked low under branches.
We drank in the sun
and counted long-forgotten snake skins
left on the mossy banks.

How could we know the shedding of skins
were part of River's prophecy to us then?

How could we know
we would become cartographers
of the backwaters
of the infinite within?

A Midnight Form of Transport

-Ring One-

The travel tonight
was not what we expected.
A shake of a six-ring shakujō[16]
opened up a doorway
to the Three Worlds of Knowing.

-Ring Two-

Backward
backward
along time's Great Spiral
backward
backward
the Gates of Seeing
were revealed.

-Ring Three-

Lured like hungry salmon
back, back,
back to the swirling memory pools

---

16 Shakujō, sometimes called a "sounding staff", is a Buddhist ringed staff used by traveling monks and Buddhist hermits, especially in Japan. The jingling sound of the shakujō scares away predators in wild places and was sometimes a formidable weapon against bandits. It is sometimes utilized as a shamanic instrument by practitioners of various forms of Japanese mountain shamanism even today.

where things forgotten are restored;
where heavy weights of karma
are finally put down.

-Ring Four-

My first stop was to memories
of my sunlight-delighted self.
My Sunlight-Delighted Self
basking in summer's warm glow.
Basking in a sense of adventure,
a sense of arrival,
a sense of welcome and perfection
before a great childhood wound
had been cleaved.

-Ring Five-

Another deep flow
of crystalline memory
birds on the wing,
laughter, a sweet flowing river,
explaining to a child
the mystery of tadpoles.

Long languid days
exploring orchards,
mystified.
Fiery shrieks as webworms
were burned in the hot wavering air.

-Ring Six-

Another gateway called me back;
this time to a life before this one.

I can see your jet-black hair pulled back,
shimmering in the autumn sunlight.

Your obi[17] the color of fresh peaches, the red of turning leaves.
The clip-clop clip-clop clack of your wooden geta on the path.
The near-final songs of the cicada buzzing, clicking as we walked.

I remember how it felt to walk beside you
your small frame edging up the path
like a bright flower flowing down a stream.

The delight in your eyes
shining like sunlight.
The leaves rustling
as the wind flowed through
like an invisible silk scarf
getting caught on the branches.

Your breathing
my breathing
the forest breathing
together
One.

---

17 Obi: The sash or belt used in traditional Japanese dress to tie silk kimono, cotton yukata,
work clothes, or martial arts uniforms. Some obi are plain and utilitarian. Other obi are highly
decorative with elaborate patterns and rich colors for formal dress.

We passed a wandering mendicant that day.

You smiled and bowed
as did he.

You asked for a blessing.
He obliged
and bowed again
a one-handed half-gassho[18]
aimed from his heart to yours.

You and I
could have spent years
beside a sunlit window together
but we left that life as strangers.

Until now,
I haven't been able
to put that down.

---

18 Gassho is a hand position used as a gesture of blessing, greeting, and reverence in Buddhist tradition. A full-gassho is a mudra of two hands placed together palm-to-palm. A half-gassho is frequently used in China and Japan. In this case, a single hand is held up at the level of the heart as a person bows.

Ikkyū's Final Vision

for Sengikumaru, in his voice

I must admit
last night
I yearned for the "cloud bed" of Lady Mori.[19]

Even now, separated by lifetimes, I am haunted by her eyes.
They shimmered and glowed and changed colors in the shifting light.
White like pearls in sunshine.
Blue-gray on days with snow.
Soft jade on rainy days in spring and summer.
Sparkling amber-gold on nights with poetry, saké,
candlelight, love-play.

I miss her hands
her curves
her laughter
her sing-song speech.
Spooning around her in winter; her rump like a sweet peach.
The way her blind eyes would gaze down
as her fingers plucked the strings of her koto[20].
Ancient songs flowed from her hands
as if they arrived from some unknown heaven.

---

19 Ikkyu Sojun was a highly unorthodox Zen master in 13th-century Japan. He eschewed
institutionalized Zen, became a hermit, and is depicted as being fond of both saké and visiting
courtesans and parlor girls. In time, Ikkyu would meet his great love, the blind musician Lady
Mori, who inspired many of his poems.
20 Koto: A Japanese 13-stringed instrument similar to the Chinese zheng, Korean gayageum,
and Vietnamese dan tranh. Considered the national instrument of Japan.

Elegant, regal, parasol in hand—
her graceful way of walking was like watching a ghost
an unfolding dream
a drifting cloud
a bright flower petal floating by in the river of time.

Here, now, a different life than before,
a different "deathbed" altogether,
I gaze up at a picture of Amida Buddha on the wall.

Multi-colored threads drape down from the image to my weak and
trembling hands.
It is soon my time to go again
but my heart-mind is still bound by the red thread.

I wonder,
does my Lady Mori wait for me?
Is the way to the Pure Land finally open?
Will I make it across the vast water to the Other Shore,
or return to this earthly plane of strife and suffering again?

Years. Who's counting?

Walk Not in Haste

Sitting here
before a steaming kettle of memories,
allowing them to rise and fall
and pass away as they rush forward,
the path is illuminated.

The lid is rattling
announcing
the song of the season
loud and clear.

Something new
is being cooked into existence.

A quiet step
into the Bright-Darkness
and it is revealed.

The Festival of Kimonos Falling Loose is over for now.

Courtesans and moon-gazers
jesters and poets
lovers and dreamers
are sharing a final embrace
before heading home.

They're closing screens and blinds,
getting their houses in order.

The small commotion you hear out in the garden
is not a child playing,
but a man gathering a few simple things,
preparing to follow the dragon's tail
up into the mountains
for another season of silence.

Instructions From Kenshō

Under dawn spruce trees
soaking in steaming water
So, this is rebirth!

Sit Like A Mountain
Breathe Like A Forest
Flow Like A River

Unguarded
Without Armor
Move Through the World Open-Hearted

Out of Season

Sometimes
I watch old samurai movies
simply because
in the depths of winter
I need to hear the sound
of noonday cicadas
and night frogs again.

Two Haiku

autumn cicada
serves as a mindfulness bell
how fleeting this life

roofers on the roof
like enormous crows pecking
me: a hiding worm

Land-Listening
for David Abram[21]

First, before entering,
you stop and pay homage
at the Juniper Shrine.

Then, the swaying Linden says:
"Come on in.
The air is just fine.
Leave the world of red dust behind."

A thousand steps in and the dry, sandy loam
starts telling stories of rains yet to come.

You look at the earth
and know it is beneath you
but swear you're seeing clouds forming there
despite the bright blue sky.

Grandfather Pine
points to his grandchildren below
and says:

---

21 This poem has a dual inspiration—a recent summer walk in which I was reminded of a
memory from 20 years ago. I had the great honor of meeting author, cultural ecologist, and
performance artist David Abram on a swaying boat in the Inside Passage of Alaska. Most of us
were sea-sick, but David didn't miss a beat as he slid in a chair, back and forth on stage, while
telling stories about the proper way to listen to birdsong.

"Look at all their new yellow tassels.
Soon the rain will come to wash them clean,
and they'll start off the Spring all fresh and green."

At the Honeysuckle Gate, croakers and chirpers
second the stories of Old Pine in their own way.

"Any moment now, Any moment now,
Any moment now, Any, Any, Any..."
"Any moment now, Any moment now,
Any moment now, Any, Any, Any..."

And then you hear it.

The western thunder.

The Flower in the Mountain

There is a flower waiting to bloom.
You have to travel to it to help it along.

It needs lots of water
but not just any water

pure water
like river-water dreaming itself.

It needs plenty of light
but not just any light

the kind of radiance absorbed
from the energy of a soul-brightening place.

It needs plenty of air
but not just any air

clean air of open space
flowing and constant
so it can move and sway
and strengthen its roots.

You cannot reach this rare mountain flower
relying on your usual avenues.

The path is long and winding,
sometimes dark, stormy, rocky,
but nothing compares to the views.

Like all pilgrimage routes
it is best to purify yourself
and not carry unnecessary weight;
but if you do, rest assured,
the natural wisdom of the energy-body
will off-load what does not serve you
for your travels the final way up.

The flower is housed in an invisible temple.
The path to the temple starts at the base of your spine.
Go at your own pace.
There is no timeline.

You are the mountain.
You are the path.
You are the Limitless Samadhi[22] Flower
that has been waiting for you all along.

---

22 Samadhi is a Sanskrit term shared by many dharmic and yogic traditions including Hinduism, Buddhism, Jainism and Sikhism, and refers to a state of meditative absorption, stillness, one-pointedness of mind.

Re-Entering the Forest

I look back and see now
I have only ever been a moist beak
pecking at the egg shell wall of tomorrow.

A seed-pod snapping open in each moment,
sending runners scurrying after sunlight.

This road I have been on
is now a sundial turning;
a relinquishing all holds and holding;
becoming a silent breathing compass again.

There is something bittersweet about letting go;
about parting from anyone or anything that holds memory.

But it is Spring.
The weather is nice outside tonight.

I put my writing utensils away for the rest of the season
and take back up
the old practices
of the Forest-Sitting Religion.

Acknowledgments

With gratitude to the wayfarers and deadbolt poets.
You know who you are.

Deep thanks to family and spirit-family.
You know who you are too.

Many thanks also to Steve Roach, Robert Rich, Forrest Fang, Byron Metcalf, Alio Die, Roy Mattson, Michael Stearns, Alcvin Ryūzen Ramos, Jeffrey Ericson Allen of the Chronotope Project, Loren Nerell, Vi-An Diep, and Calexico for all of the sonic medicine indispensable from my practice of poetry.

About the Author

Born into a family of artists, clergy, cowboys, fly fishermen, and poets, Frank LaRue Owen studied for a decade with a New Mexican wise woman and wilderness guide who guided him through a "curriculum" of Zen meditation, dream-tracking, poem-incubation, and earth-spirit work in the mountains, forests, and arroyos of Colorado and New Mexico. Influenced by the *Chan* (Zen), Daoist, and Pure Land hermit-poet traditions, American eco-poetry, and the wider human lineage of cross-cultural mystical poetry, Owen's poems are shaped by dreams, the seasons, diverse landscapes, myth-lines in the deeper strata of ancestral memory, and experiences with a practice he calls "pure land dreaming." Owen's other poetry and writing can be found at: purelandpoetry.com

HOMEBOUND PUBLICATIONS

Ensuring that the mainstream isn't the only stream.

At Homebound Publications, we publish books written by independent voices for independent minds. Our books focus on a return to simplicity and balance, connection to the earth and each other, and the search for meaning and authenticity. Founded in 2011, Homebound Publications is one of the rising independent publishers in the country. Collectively through our imprints, we publish between fifteen to twenty offerings each year. Our authors have received dozens of awards, including: *Foreword Reviews'* Book of the Year, Nautilus Book Award, Benjamin Franklin Book Awards, and Saltire Literary Awards. Highly-respected among bookstores, readers and authors alike, Homebound Publications has a proven devotion to quality, originality and integrity.

We are a small press with big ideas. As an independent publisher we strive to ensure that the mainstream is not the only stream. It is our intention at Homebound Publications to preserve contemplative storytelling. We publish full-length introspective works of creative non-fiction as well as essay collections, travel writing, poetry, and novels. In all our titles, our intention is to introduce new perspectives that will directly aid humankind in the trials we face at present as a global village.

Printed in the USA
CPSIA information can be obtained
at www.ICGtesting.com
JSHW080002150824
68134JS00021B/2225